FROM HURT
TO HEALING

A Collection of Thought-Provoking Poetry

Compiled by Sarah Hall and John Latimer

…the past abuse, will be put to use!!!

A selection of authors have shared their hearts,
borne out of their experiences of pain and healing,
in order to help you on your own healing journey.

Contributors

Mr. Anderson
Sarah Hall
Darren Jones
River Jordan
Stephen King
Cliff Latimer
Jack Latimer
John Latimer
Jason Scarborough

ISBN 978 0 86071 867 3

A Commissioned Publication Printed by

MOORLEYS
Print, Design & Publishing
info@moorleys.co.uk · www.moorleys.co.uk

Valued

To feel loved and valued
Appreciated
Know that your offering's
Substantiated

Light in the darkness
Bright shining
Warmth in the cold days
Silver lining

Abused

Abused as a child which I did not know,
Until a family member told me so.

The thoughts of what happened and what should I do?
Was really quite harrowing and hurtful too

I classed him as my uncle, as I grew by his side.
He showed me the way to Heaven through my Lord and
Saviour Jesus Christ.

He showed me the way to life, but didn't want to pay the price.
To deny this life and walk in Him, the One that paid for all his sin.

Because you've been abused, people think you would go that
way too?
But praise be to God I did not follow his way.

The Lord knows my heart and He knows I would not think
that too,
Who could hurt a child innocent and true?

I forgave my abuser, he chose his path.
But remember Satan did not have the last laugh.

My abuser led me to Jesus who paid for all my sin,
Who cleansed me wholly and washed me from within.

Next time you judge, remember too,
These things could have happened to you.

I could not remember what happened to me,
But I thank my God for setting me free.

Jesus

He carried me a lifetime, solved problems showed he cared
Gave me inner vision, to the road He had prepared
Tended hurts so many, gave His very blood
Took my sins my darkness left, my doubts He understood
He stroked my hair when sleeping, a heartfelt inner peace
The Lamb of God beside me, to touch upon the fleece
He walked with me in footsteps, He cried the tears of I
He laughed within my joyous times; He's never passed me by
He nurtured in our group today, poured Spirit we could feel
His vision entered Michael, gave wisdom touch to heal
His promises believeth will always come to bear
His love for all is endless, He leads to golden stair
Trust in the Lord He'll feed us, we will never go without
Our praises raise the rooftop, sing glory Jesus shout
He gives us joy and laughter, He cradles in our lows
His presence is so paramount, his guidance truth He shows
His warmth could melt a glacier, warm heart that once so iced
We claim Him Lord our Master, His title Jesus Christ

AMEN

Bless you Lord

Satan

The enemy always wants to condemn you, you know it's
always true
To make you look inside your head, to try to make you blue
The thoughts you think are not always you, but can that be true?
You see he will place a thought within your mind and say it's
really you
In truth it's what he's done, trying to ground you
But I am only mortal? I walk upon this ground, how can I get
above this mortal shroud?
The secret is in your imagination it's just a spark you see, to see
yourself with King of Kings above this place you be
So look to He the true One, where all light is found at source
To bathe in His light of lights and soar where eagles soar
Don't be confined by this world, look to the one to come
To see celestial beings and then we will have fun
You see that's where Satan once was with our Father and Lord
But sin was in his heart, to take the life from all
But God had a rescue plan before the throes of time
He spoke Himself into existence was born by virgin birth
To make the way back to you, with His time here on earth
Satan already knew this, so tempted you with all his power
But You knew that was not the Way, or your chosen hour
You died a death 3 years after that upon a cross of shame
To save us your people, for you to truly gain
To make us Born again by your Spirit from above, not to be
confined by this passing mortal frame
So next time when you're tempted to act upon some sin
Remember you are born from above no need to be bound in sin

Acceptance

I come into your presence
Just as I am
No fear of oppression
It's never a sham

Your love and acceptance
Of me, is sure
I know that repentance
Will keep my heart pure

Your love unconditional
Your grace, without measure
No need for additional
Good works or pleasure

Your love overwhelms me
There's nothing I need
Your grace helping me be
Forgiven and freed

Shattered Being

The avenue of love I have closed within my mind
The word of love is never used in time was left behind
Love broke me of my everything my body once erect
Love tore the very being strewn, in science labs dissect
Laid bare no shield of hatred my body shrunk to cower
Emptied out my life force, in none I found empower

I crawled away to lick my wounds, I hid in darkest thought
I listened to the whispers there, this murder should I ought?
I crept away still further my children left behind
I cried to God have mercy, kill me send me blind
Take my heart still hurting, close my thought be still
Give me silence to my ears, evaporate my will

For now, I've built a person new, from pieces scattered round
I clung to people's intellect, I trained this thought profound
I built an ivory tower, one span of life neglect
Now what you see of nine years late, a man to stand erect
You ask so is this total, whole, complete, intact?
There's corners and some doorways closed, a few cataract

But one day in my future a dawn one day shall rise
In love let near but once again, to look into her eyes

Openness

Could you undress in front of all, use personal disclosure?
Find strength through your serenity,
be nude just total exposure
Could you bare your soul to peoples there?
to find your sense of worth?
Could you trust in your surroundings?
let your feelings feel fresh air?
To listen to one's inner self, to respect and give a care

Could you lend your voice to others, to find their inner peace?
And so, to give your heart and soul for them to feel release
This prize you hold for all the earth just sense that's if you can
Then alter ego to the fore, then you are a man
Could you allow the tears of hurt to flow and form a trace?
Then when this is done in trust there is no pain disgrace
Could you show your naked feelings bold?
to an audience unknown?
Then all the pains you felt my friend
will be judged and so atone

Anxiety

In the middle of nothing
Heart starts to race
Hands feel all shaky
You start to need space

Walls are enclosing
Struggling to breathe
Need to escape
Panic rising beneath

Take a deep breath now
It will all be okay
Centre your mind
And then start to pray

Heartbeat slows down
Hands start to steady
You're grounded again
To move you are ready

Defences

I can't let those people deep inside to decide if I am sane
I can't let them see the agony that hatred or my pain
I just keep things locked away inside, none hitherto I trust
I'll use conditioned reflexes like belittle spite and lust
I can't let them wander freely, in the inner space of mind
They could empty all protective shields,
my energy they'll bind

I'm panicking they're at my door, their knocking, can't come in
I don't need help from none at all, to me your doing sin
Look I'll go to church I'll be good boy, don't put upon my head
Then as electric current dies, I feel like zombie dead
Then as the line proceeds in tow,
to the tablets you've prescribed

As some memories appear from past, this poem has described
The place of rest and tranquil sights, in hospital for insane
If folk just stall the growth of mind, then what in life's to gain?
Electric shock and tablets harsh, for a body raked with strife
You may as well lop off my head with a spoon
or near blunt knife

Time to Heal

It's time for your healing
The layers are peeling
No longer concealing
The way you are feeling

Each day you are dealing
Your memories revealing
The truth it's demeaning
The way you are feeling

Some days you are squealing
It's rarely appealing
The thoughts are repealing
The way you are feeling

And now as you're kneeling
Experience your healing
It's no longer stealing
The truth you are feeling

White Lines

Paranoia is waiting just outside my door, as I sniff the gear
appropriate as the sweat begins to pour
Paranoia is my friend in tow this second half to I, no feelings
for the love or loss no reasons for to cry
Paranoia is the gift of sense it keeps one on one's toes,
and as the years
tick by in moments the void expands and grows
Paranoia bites the ass it feeds it knows no bounds or gait; it
sneaks around a mind to pounce it sniggers there in wait
Paranoia learns tricks of trade survival and the rest; it states
that one cannot be wrong people are horrid you're the best
Paranoia gives one life instilled but to look at how much cost,
to look back o'er the years it's reigned
and look how much one's lost
Paranoia waiting at my door unless I make the change, I feel
that if I alter course my mind will not derange
Paranoia gives me space to think let go that hold secure, please
I beg release my soul on bended knee implore
I see I can divulge my fears to the world once feared with hate, and
Paranoia is there to pounce, ambush lays in wait
Paranoia is a part of I and to seize my mind it blinds, but left
alone the drugs of choice those little silver lines
Then truth could enter in my being and give me purpose hope,
just leave the lady amphets and of course that stinking dope
And then relax to see and sense to breathe exhale and so
inhale, to ponder thoughts and put to rhyme
at least to tell one's tale
Now as my life she ebbs and flows I ponder where and why,
then peek at losses I've incurred and morosely breathe a sigh

Show Me My Fears

Show me my fears
Help me overcome
Lord, dry my tears
I don't want to be numb

Fears based on lies
Show me the truth
Then these fears will die
I don't need any proof

Your love is real
Your grace overwhelming
This pain that I feel
The fears, they are melting

Into your love
Into your grace
Things from above
Put fears in their place

The Government

The governments not bothered,
for the drugs you pay top dollar
They've no interest in the Ganja seeds,
the amount that's finally cropped
No scruples for transmitted sex, or veins injected (popped)
The government's not bothered, of the quality of the gear
So, when a death of child's read out, they apologise sincere
We try they claim confronted, of the rings of crime to bust
Then seized drugs go a-missing, the law who can trust?
The government's not bothered, just scrawl your little X
They will con you with their speeches, with a Scholar'd text
They can't worry when you're starving,
emotion shown they'd fret
As parents look into an open grave, with such remorse, regret
The government's not bothered, if you work or are idle
They're not interested in reality, if you're sane or suicidal
They will promise you your worldly goods,
your dreams your finest hour
Installed their quotes are worthless, still they are in power
The governments not bothered,
five years they puff their breast
When election comes again, they will retire to feathered nest
They have no inclination, of the thugs upon your door
Get thine own protection, is just a dialogue for the poor
The government's not bothered, of canny that we have toked
The opium, the weed, or coke or the dragon chased so smoked
This government as all before, will beg keep using drugs
So governed by the government,
no revolt to come (what mugs)

Accidents

I killed okay an accident, with blows and kicks to head,
A skull was cracked an accident, upon the floor he bled
Glazed eyes as I was pulled away, but an accident ensued
Fixation on my prey with red, an accident unglued.

I ran away from melee, an accident for four
An accident in years gone by, but hurt for many more
Always temper flaring an accident in wait
Spawning lying in my thoughts an accident to date

Crawling lying spitting an accident in truth
An accident you coppers and no other there be proof
An accident I scream at you, as prison bars I see
An accident at birth there was, the accident was me

An accident I tell you, I was down depressed so blue
But when I look into my mind, an accident not true

Moving on

Hurt and betrayed
The decision is made
I'm not looking back
The path has been laid

Letting go of the past
Moving on to new things
With the people I trust
Who will not put me last

It is hard and it hurts
But I know that it's right
Time to heal, and rebuild
And get rid of the dirt

To be whole and restored
And with people who care
Letting go of the others
Trusting you now, my Lord

Running in Circles

I've been running away most my life
Trying to escape my haunting past
Now I'm starting to get really tired
Surely much longer this can't last

For half my life I existed outside
Of normality in perpetual torment
But there's only one to blame for this
I couldn't allow it to relent

As I believed it was deserved
For the callous things I'd done
For the lies I told & lives I'd ruined
I never realised my decency had gone

I was an empty vessel a hollow soul
Beaten, broken, battered and vacant
The lights were on but no one was home
Trapped in the abyss my exit so distant

I wandered the streets as a figureless ghoul
Searching for more to destroy me
For my next escape from this hell
The sharp sting of my enemy my only release

The warmth that followed sent me into the clouds
But temporary it was and soon I was back
Hunting for the next one hopefully my last
For I hated myself I prayed for death prayed for black

But death never released me
I had to fight till the end
Because someone out there Loved me
Finally Love that wasn't pretend

I'll heal you and guide you
I'll pick you pick you up when you fall
I'll show you the path that's true &
A Love that's pure

Just open up your heart to me
A new life is yours be pure
I will never hurt you or bring you down
Just open up your eyes you'll see

You are a king without his crown
I will give you one of beaming light &
Everlasting life through me
So stand up and proud you're free my child &

Battle on with all your might
The day I stood up free & clean
With that power by my side
Was my proudest day yet, it broke my heart

From all the pain I held inside
But long ago that day now seems
Yet my pain will not give up
Apologies I've gave but still I feel it burn

But I won't back down I won't be corrupt
I will fight till it's gone from my soul
I will walk strong & faithful
Until I reach the point I am finally whole

A Play On Words

So skilled is error at imitating truth,
it takes a sharp eye these days to spot it!

Language is the sheath words fit into!

Out of sight out of mind, but what if what's troubling you
cannot be put out of sight, then it remains in your mind!

Fight like a brave or live like a slave!

No one can say both yes and no in the same breath, so, let your
yes be yes and your no be no!

What they built with their bare hands thousands of years ago,
we still can't do today!

One heart made to suffer, one heart made to crawl, one heart
made to be broken, one heart made to fall!

No one knows if they have a next breath to take!

You think you're running the show but it's running you!

Fame doesn't always bring fortune,
and fortune doesn't always bring fame!

Sometimes the best way to know what a thing is, is to firstly
know what it isn't!

You get dealt it, and that's the deal!

Atmosphere

The atmosphere is suffocating
Life draining
Joy taming
I can't breathe
I can't cry
Gasping for air
Just want to die
Nowhere to run
Nowhere to hide

Then I remember
Who is by my side?
In God I find my refuge
In God my heart is safe
In God I find my healing
And that my friends is huge

The atmosphere is changing
As on God's strength I lean
I stand for truth and justice
Refuse to be unseen

The Spirit is life giving
Joy making
Fear taking
The Spirit is thirst quenching
Living waters
Gods' daughter

I find my truth in Him alone
In Him my worth is sure
He stands me on the solid rock
Abundant life - unlocks!

The Hardest Word For Me

I've said goodbye so many times
Some have been easy and others not so
I've had tears in my eyes and lumps in my throat
From the ones causing heartache as I've watched you go

The incredible sadness felt in my heart
To watch loved ones disappear right before my eyes
To hold onto their last words and whispers
Sometimes so difficult inside my soul dies

To have to watch as they walk away
Taking with them a small piece of my being
Smashing through the armour I wear
To protect me from the world and the pain I keep seeing

I've watched you leave and I've watched you die
I've watched as the one I love so dearly
Gets stripped away and the beauty so angelic
Withers and fades, eyes once bright and bleary

This one word has made me fall apart
And also made me stronger than ever
It's crumbled my heart and tears have stung my eyes
Having to say this word too much "goodbye is forever"

But sometimes forever it just has to be
No more broken heartedness it can cause
And your mind can be set free
Then your soul can fly high like an eagle it soars
So to quote an old song

Goodbye my lover and goodbye my friend
Just know that you'll always be remembered
Somewhere in my heart till the end

Because even the goodbyes that hurt deep inside
The ones you try to forget in your soul still hide
And bury them you try you will not succeed
No matter how much you ask and you beg and you plead

These are the ones that make us so strong
That give us our drive and passion to push on
So store them inside and learn from them please
They will make you a warrior
And a better life you will see

So goodbye my lovers and goodbye my friends
You'll always have a place in my heart
Right until the bitter end

Affirmation

To be affirmed
of grace to learn

A sense of belonging
This love, a prolonging

To be accepted
My desire pre-empted
My mistakes not preventing
His love unrelenting

Earth Suit

To walk upon this plain called earth a face a form, disguise
Then watch as Spirit soars to heights a transformation such surprise
One sees but he does nothing, falters in his task
Just listen to this beating globe and in her aura bask

Stretch out those fingers sense your world; drop inside your form
Understand immortal being, let one's mind explode so swarm
Delve into space and planets roam, bend time and inner realm
Imagine all you can and more as a captain at one's helm

Belief in one's transcendence goes sight this inner zone
Through portals travel spiral voids take in the maelstrom cone
This confinement that you're feeling, leave behind let it spoil
Go further than you've ever gone to suns to seethe and boil

Forgiveness and Apologies

So I've hit a part of my life
Where I asked God to forgive
To forgive me for my wrongdoings
And I have to do this so I can live
Live my new life the way I should
Not how "I believe it should go"
And not "I'll do it if only I could"
Well now I can and say it I shall
I am sorry to all those I've hurt
And I'm sorry for all those who hurt me
So here goes I hope I get them all
But hey we will see...

I am sorry I deceived you
I am sorry I lied
I am sorry I didn't push you
I'm sorry I pushed too hard
I'm sorry I disappointed you
I'm sorry I let you down
I'm sorry if I gave up too soon
I'm sorry if I didn't give up sooner
I'm sorry I distracted you
I'm sorry I didn't distract you enough
I'm sorry if I gave up on me
I'm sorry if I gave up on you
I'm sorry I didn't put you first
I'm sorry I didn't come first
I'm sorry life didn't go as planned
I'm sorry life went astray

I'm sorry if I didn't love you enough
I'm sorry I loved you too much
I'm sorry I couldn't give you more
And I'm sorry I gave you too much

Sorry is a hard word to say
Things don't always work out the right way
Sometimes you end up getting mad
And others you just end up way too sad

To apologise sincerely is a difficult thing
We don't always do it from a sincere heart
And that's why sometimes the words sting
So always be honest right from the start

If God can forgive me then how can I not
Yet to forgive myself now that's another matter
The things I have done and words I have said
Have caused pain undeserved and hearts to shatter

So I say these words from a place inside
From my heart so sincere it's plagued me
Chased my dreams until now revealed
To apologise for my wrongs is now my plea

Please accept my words as true from within
And know I meant no harm or malice
I hope you can forgive so I can be free
Also I hope my words aren't too late
And these things I have written you'll see
No response is required I just had to get them out
To each and every one I've hurt
And from the bottom of my heart
"I am truly sorry, please forgive me."

Who am I?

Am I defined by all I've seen?
The places I have been?
The highs and lows
The way life goes
On who I've had to lean?

Or is it in what God has said?
The things He thinks of me?
The love and truth
It's in His word
There, written for all to see

I am His child and I believe
His love I will receive
I choose to hear
Overcome the fear
I am loved for He loves me

Self Worth

That God thought I was worth it
He came and died for me
While I may think that I'm unfit
He came to set me free

Free from all the lies I heard
Lies that I believed
My failures left him undeterred
My peace He has retrieved

Now help me Lord, to love myself
to see what I am worth
it's hard to know and give oneself
The love we do deserve

You Paid the Price for Me

You lived your life and died to set us free
I'll pray and believe you'll see
Your worthiness gifted me and now I'm blessed and free
Your parables guided me with you I'm worthy, believers see

Priceless free you paid the price for me
You gave your life for me
When I heard you call my heart let you in
Now free of sin, eyes open this is my pledge to you

My heart is true I'll give my life to you
Lord I'm calling out your name I'm born again and I proclaim
Sins are forgotten in your name.
Lord I'm not the same how Holy is your name.

In the Lord I am set free
You're always there for me. My conscience is set free
You're always there for me blessed for all to see
Your Spirit lives in me you died to set me free
You paid the price for me

You paid the price for me
I'll pray and believe you'll see
You gave your life for me
Sins are forgotten in your name
In the Lord I am set free

No Escape

I hold my breath
Wait for death
Out of misery
My only delivery

I feel so low
Things are slow
My life, a nightmare
Things I can't share

Trapped in this life
Always in strife
No way to escape
You've kept me in shape

You Chose The Cross

You refuse to let hate live while love dies
Only you can see where my future lies
You resurrected for all to see
You chose the cross our sins set free

A crown of thorns that you withstood
For the shining light of what is good
The book of life for us to follow
Teaching us your perfect morals

You chose the cross to complete the Trinity
All ancient prophecies fulfilled so diligently
Only to see you rise again
If not now I'll see you then

When you take me in your arms
With the angels beside you at your throne
Our prayers are answered we can see
You chose the cross our sins are set free

The Battle

It's a battle in the mind the
Dark side of human stealth

But maybe it's a combination of
All voices in oneself

The good the bad and ugly could
Be boxes in the brain

To carry out the bad side
Folk might think you've gone insane

The good side is so different
A picture perfect that you paint

Folk look at you and chat
A while and think that you're a saint

The ugly is a merge of both,
The devil and your God

Unearthed this combination you
Want to bury under sod

One wishes to pick the
Good box the one where all is true

To fight the ugly,
When life is just so blue

We all have choice to choose,
Which we will carry

Aim for good then the
Bad and the ugly will have to tarry

Body Language

The look in your eyes spoke volumes
The shrug of your shoulders - a shout
Your silence was loud and deafening
Of my failing, there was not a doubt

Made to feel small and useless
Like dirt on the sole of your shoe
But your words contradict, they encourage
I'm confused and not sure what to do

There are days full of joy, full of laughter
Days when the loving's so sweet
But days when we turn the next chapter
Days where I'm facing deceit

I am learning to walk upon eggshells
thinking carefully where I should tread
The thought of you getting unhappy
is something that fills me with dread

Life's Causes

Don't unlock the seething cauldron as black as pitch so dark
Listen to the terror steps, do not try to quell but hark
Do not lift the lid of life my friend open wounds in there galore
Exposed to light again from past, they are sensitive so sore
Do not open hurts abounding
do not state my rights from wrong

I will witness when I'm ready or else you'll feel my tongue
Do not undermine my intelligence with whimpers feeling low
I wander free without a care in truth I wish to know
Do not make assumption of my worth or my honesty intact
Do not look upon my form to date,
when my name's been always blacked

Do not give me advice my friend I know it all you see
I'll let you in a mind so cold, where folks did injure me
Do not tell of light within my being, I've seen the folk of God
They smile to you and hug your form, they do not give a sod
I do not want my life to date, I never wished it so
Goodbye sweet earth farewell to all, for now my heart must go

Freedom in Christ

In Christ I am free
To be the man God wants me to be
Not to wear masks and stay at home
It's God I trust not man alone
I want to go where I want and see my family
There is not freedom today!!! A reality

A virus the world fears
Going on now for nearly two years
A vaccine that will set us free
And bring back normality
If you believe that to be true
Well then, I'm sorry because I pity you

If ears can hear and eyes can see
Wake up!!! World and smell the coffee
Every year prices go up
What goes up must come down!
I am sick of this financial merry-go-round

A world of sin for you and me
Is all it has to offer me
I am free from self and normality
Because freedom in Christ has set me free

Dark Thoughts

The thoughts that plague me
Dark dark thoughts
Despair, hopelessness, fear
Dark dark thoughts

Alone and lonely, lonely and alone
Dark, dark thoughts
Better off without me
Dark, dark thoughts

Regret, sadness, pain, deep pain
Dark, dark thoughts
Never enough, doing the wrong thing
Dark, dark thoughts

As I slip into the abyss of
Dark, dark thoughts
A hand grabs mine and gently starts to pull me up
Dark, dark thoughts

A chink of light breaks into the darkness
Dark, dark thoughts
Letting go, letting God take care of
Dark, dark thoughts

Such Power

Does God speak in dreams to one, in guidance to the cause?
Does he show the word of wisdom to stride on without a pause?
Can He create a vision in words to make one see?
Then pray to Him our Father seated bended knee

Can I do His bidding wisely this flesh with all its grime?
To give Him praise abundance to note His words to rhyme
Can I teach all His forgiveness when I am but a lad?
Portray His heavenly love for all to call Him Father, Dad

When I feel a mortal being too, He a grain of sand
To show a world of violence in truth to take His hand
May I draw on His awesomeness to state His words of peace?
So, men can look beyond this realm and let the hatred cease

Bugs

It started with the sniffles
Drip drip from you know where
I sat in chair just shivering
So glum poor me, despairing
The Anadin not helping just
Fevered brow some rest
I tried to fight to no avail
I came off second best
They said at docs a virus
Said nowt that they could do
I shivered and I shook all night
My poor old feet turned blue
Hot soup is all I'd muster
From a larder dwindling fast
Some beverages with sugar sweet
And prayers that I'd outcast
They say their tiny microbes
That infiltrate one's being
No matter what their size is
The believing is the seeing
They say don't be so mardy
You'll live another day
And then they ask if I want a jab
A statement I no way
They said I'd been infected by
Some unknown with just a sneeze
It travelled on the plain of life
With a cough on mighty breeze
They said it landed in my sight
And from there it grew and grew
They said I was a baby
I'd only got a touch of the man flu

Sorry

You sit and you tell me you're sorry
You admit to the pain that you caused
But there's something not right in my spirit
Repentance should come with real change

Instead all I see is a mirror
As you copy the things that you've seen
The abuse is still there, it's just hidden
Undercover, covert and unseen

Your words are so sweet, they're like honey
Your eyes watch my face for a clue
As you plan and make real calculations
am I ever gonna know what is true?

The days are exhausting and draining
Relax is not something I do
Stay on guard, be aware of your tactics
I know I can never trust you

My Fault

We carry guilt abounding and never grant release
We search our hearts and inner thoughts
but never find our peace
One death we plead to unknown force,
why me you singled chose

Then through the years the hatred coursed the bitter seed arose
One life as boy not great or good, but tried a moral code
Running scared doubting all, could ne'er find one's abode
The wisdom sought upon the streets to mould a stronger man
Destruction of one human heart, just took some years to span

To look death in its frightening face and laugh upon its cause
To find my shelter from the cold to fight without a pause
Then find a thread of light inside to nurture it to grow
To sense to feel to kneel release and let his kingdom grow

I often look at past and now and none I'd alter change
Although at times and many more
my mind was fraught derange
My thanks I have is Christ my Lord who waited patient there
He showed me love and gratitude
and showed there's one to care

Anger

Do we feel and accept it
This anger inside?
Or hide and deny it
To ourselves have we lied?

Do we know how to handle?
These feelings of grief?
Do we think it's a scandal?
Do we have this belief?

Can we learn to express it?
In a way non destructive
Not to swallow or hide it
But to make it productive

Can we use this emotion?
To bring about change
Sometimes a commotion
Will things rearrange

Any Man

He prowls the streets unsure of his goal
A church espied could this make him whole?

He feels so damned his presence there,
A teardrop forms is there one who will care?

In search of truth and inner peace,
The fear inside it may now cease?

His question is, am I worthy lord?
What I've done is of my own accord.

Homeless, dishevelled his face upon the ground,
In Christ our Lord this man is now found.

No more deceit and lies to oneself,
No more crime so filled with stealth.

He looks to the heavens he looks above,
This man is saved through the Saviour's love.

This Man

He prowls the streets, unsure of where he heads.
He prowls the streets, unsure of where he heads.
He prowls the streets, unsure of where he heads.

The city sleeps safe in their beds.
The shadows surround him, like a silken quilt.
He shows no emotion, he runs from his guilt.
Can he be saved?

He is known by many, but no one knows him.
He lives in the shadows; his Sin life is a Sin.
He wears many masks, lets very few in.
He stumbles through life, tasting sorrow and pain.
He wants to be happy, but self-love he can't gain.

Was he born this way? No he was made.
Where is he going, what does he seek?
Does he want to be saved?

The shame overwhelms him; it tears at his soul.
He picks up his cross, repentance his goal.
He was born in the darkness, but the light he can see.
When the pain is removed, the light he will be.

Was he born this way? No, he was made.
Where is he going? What does he seek?
This man will be saved.

Born new in the spirit, his score board is clean.
The strength of that spirit, by its fruits will be seen.
Chosen by God, tempered by pain.
A man of pure heart, that's been cleared of his shame.

This Man is Saved.

Lies

Lies I've been believing
Things hidden deep within
Useless, and unworthy
You know you'll never win

Nobody can love you
Your life is such a mess
No matter what you try and do
You'll never find success

My head knows this is nonsense
I see the gifts I hold
My heart is so much slower
Not daring to be so bold

Help me as I walk this road
The path to see the truth
Discard the lies that I believed
The lies sprung from my youth

Precious Time

We look at life in a portal's the essence of one's soul
Look back in time where we were brave
and build to make us whole
I am now in my seventies look back a youngster fool
Grow up and thought a hard man, to terrify so cruel

I suppose the stages of my being were taught by father kind
Psychiatric hospitals, the ones that break one's mind
Yeah, kicked and punched from an early age,
nothing but a pawn
Then later years averse to pain watch the hatred spawn

Wading into battles strong, no remorse if hurts got bad
They said I was a lunatic or maybe once gone mad
And then a little quiet voice spoke inside my head
He asked me to apologise not cling to hatred thread
He asked if I would follow Him? Up to me, my choice
All I'd do is harken, to a storytelling voice

I listened there intently whilst sitting on His knee
He told me of the dangers front, but by my side he'll always be

Where is She?

She went away – "but where?"
I feel her presence everywhere,
She guides my feet and shows me how,
To ease the pain and stroke my brow,
She's always in my innermost thoughts,
And lifts me up when out of sorts.

To feel her near is to know such bliss,
I even imagine I feel a feathery kiss,
And when I sit around and pine
I often feel her hand in mine
It gives me strength to know she's near
She's not gone away at all – she's here!

She went away – "but where?"
I'd hear her step on every stair
She touched my face to show me how,
To bear the pain and cool my brow,
She was always there, I do recall,
And had not gone away at all.

But now I'm stood in new abode
A bungalow just up the road
I came here, but she stayed there
She's gone away again "but where?"
But when I climb that heavenly stair,
I'll find her, for I know – "she's there!"

First Meeting

I've not gone I just reside in a different space
A sigh last breath retires from the human race

My spirit soars as I'd always spied
A floating light, no need to hide

I watch over my kin in their visual life
I wish them to carry no strife

I see my Lord in light and splendour
He clothes my soul and holds me tender

He asks me questions all in His Grace
About my time in the Human race

I answer freely no need deceit
Upon His mount we finally meet

I told him of my troubles and strife
How stupid to lose my lovely wife

He dries my chest no need for tears
No argument, no pensive fears

His Kingdom realm we walk in tow
No rush, no bustle, just nice and slow

I learn my values and one other thing
He's always been there my Jesus and King

Let it Cease

The tears that flow
As I let go
Of all the pain
The hurt, I know

Memories buried
Deep inside
Now these feelings
Won't subside

Lord bring healing
Lord bring peace
Take this pain
Let it cease

Return of the King

I've gotten so used to the darkness
I've began to call it home
Constantly falling I stumble along
Like some worthless mindless drone

But I have seen a light
Somewhere off deep in the distance
So I'm fumbling through the chaos
With the devil it'll be my last dance

I fight off hordes of demons
All wanting the weight of my flesh
But I refuse to give in this time
I'm back on my feet and starting afresh

I've danced with the devil and
I've eaten at his table
I've swallowed his lies
Telling me I'm not able

But I say to the devil
With new vigour in my soul
I'm no longer your plaything
A new life is my goal

So now I look in the mirror
On a fill of visions twisted and dark and
A light shines now brightly
Giving hope to my new walk

Now as my pen hits my paper
A new sensation in my heart
A lost warmth returns
I've finally found my spark

I feel fresh and renewed
Full of gratitude and Love
For my supporters and listeners &
From the presence from above

I am healing yet hurting
Broken-hearted, still fixing
But I have faith in my power
Gifted down from the heavens and

In my darkest hour
I know He will be there
No matter how broken
I know He will still care

So here I go again on this path
To where I don't yet know
But no matter where it leads
With hope and faith I'll go

So goodbye my old friend despair and
Hello to my new friend desire
You help me to heal and
New life you inspire

So onwards I go with the light in my hand
No longer on the edge of the abyss do I stand
I stand proud and inspired
To walk my promised land

Touch of Jesus

When I'm feeling unclean
In the wrong and ashamed
When I'm feeling unseen
And I'm taking the blame

For the things that have happened
Though I wasn't at fault
For the way I've been treated
And the sexual assault

I will reach out and touch you
The one who is pure
I know what you can do
Your word makes me sure

Wholeness and healing
You bring to my life
You deal with the feelings
You deal with the strife

I trust you Lord Jesus
You bring us to truth
And I know that you see us
In our old age and youth

Gentle Lord

He watches from our onset, and with patience there He'll wait
He sees the spite thrown inside out, but ne'er does He berate
He gives us choice to follow He, but does not scare condemn
He feeds our souls if we believe, like nourishment from root to stem
He hears one waiting asking why; he raps upon our door
He holds one close and carries mind, as one's tears begin to fall

His footprints in the sands of life, mark a time He once did carry
Then as the pain fades in our hearts, we loiter darkness tarry
We go to Christ so filled with guilt, with sin we ask to cleanse
We walk with thee we talk with thee,
say our prayers our psalms Amens

Then stride we do on open ground, again we feel gait
And left behind just put on hold, our gentle Lord will wait
He'll smile with thee in happy times, and weep when one is sad
He'll tap upon your window pane,
when in thought one thinks one's mad

He'll aid one on his journey, to hopes and dreams galore
And all He asks our pledge to self,
is your word is true and pure

The Call to Forgive

The call to forgive
In harmony live
Seems too high a cost
When you have been crossed

The pain does it matter?
Your heart has been shattered
The betrayal is brutal
Your efforts are futile

To hold onto this hurt
To cling to the dirt
An easier choice?
Ignore the small voice?

Inside you will suffer
The road will get tougher
As hate eats you up
You drink from the cup

Bitter and bereft now
Is it time to allow
Forgiveness to flow
Though it may be slow

As you learn to let go
Of what brought you low
Hold onto the light
You'll get through the night

It's time for your healing
The layers are peeling
No longer concealing
The way you are feeling

The call to forgive
In harmony live
The best choice to make
The best road to take

The Truth

Truth is how one hears it, in gossip form harsh tongue
Whispers in a corridor, no not at all I'm wrong
Truth is in believing, the wit of one's own girth
The fragility of prospect the outcome of one's birth
Truth is indescribable a fragment piece of news
To snigger huddled corner what ere may it amuse

Harken come yet closer let me whisper in one's ear
The truth is but an outcome, chatter who is near
Outspoken all and sundry everyone knows who
Let's wait and be so vengeful we'll snarl and hiss and boo
Truth is masquerading to tiptoe round and round
Truth is where the heart is, but nearly never found

But whatever hears about one whether happy or so blue
The gossips argue daily, whatever they say is true
Don't try to ever convince them, they know that they are right
A huddled group of gossips are worthy of their spite
The spoken word is varied it alters day by day
And whomever is the speaker on the weak they stalk their prey

A cover story that's for sure no truth of human race
Yet all on earth are truthful that is to someone's face
Some skid on truth supposing the darkness of desire
When will these folk acknowledge fault and call the truth a liar?
The truth we feel is generated as they slander smirk and sup
Their truth is so important so, it's whatever they make up

I Dared Say No

I take a breath and brace myself
For what is now to come
I know that he'll be making sure
I pay for what I've done

The penance will be subtle
A mood, some silence, a look
the result will be effective
My confidence is shook

I will know it's my place not to question
Or ask for my needs to be met
Instead I must curb my expression
Be thankful for the crumbs that I get

The sin I committed what was it?
It must have been awful and bad?
The thing that I did, that I shouldn't?
I said no, that's what made him so mad

Freedom From The Other Life

Take your eyes off the Lord and what do you see?
A life surrounded by misery

The flesh cannot satisfy and never will
So why do we try to fulfil?
A vessel that will only ever want more,
What a waste of this life and what God has in store.

Look to Him, He knows the way
And from His path never stray

He will never forsake you
Or leave you on your own
Be bold, be strong His power is unknown
He will move through us His power to display

So take them stones up, on your path today,
Walk in Him because you want it so
Not to earn but let his grace bestow.

Set your face like flint this day,
To achieve His will in your life today.

Walk each day with your Lord in sight,
To crush the darkness of this life.
Don't let your flesh tempt you so,
But walk in Christ and let His Love grow.

Don't listen to the enemy's lies,
You're seated above these earthly skies

In Christ above and in no other,
For in His Love we will discover,
How to truly love and care for each other.

Witnessed

The lamb of God was murdered
But then it was His choice
Millenniums may pass on by
But still we hear His voice
They stripped Him of His dignity
Impaled thorns upon His crown
He did not plead for mercy
His brow there was no frown

They whipped his flesh unmerciful
Until His bones showed white
The crowds that cheered in order
His halo still shone bright
In death they rolled a stone in place
That none could enter in
He'd died to be our Saviour and
Cast out all our sin

He rose and went to heaven
To sit beside His Lord
The trinity was set in place
The pen is mightier than the sword
I pray that you'll forgive my sins
And they are many fold
Then look my Lord and Master
Your story has been told

Open Your Heart

Today is the day
Let hope and love in
Soften the way
Allow love to begin

Unlocking the door
Gently easing it open
Trembling and shaking
Scared it's too broken

The pain of the past
Your heart has been torn
Could stop you from sharing
And make you uncaring

It's time to be brave
Be sure who you are
Allow love to awaken
Despite all the scars

Tomorrow

I'm going to die tomorrow with what God only knows
In agony and moaning mess in the final of death throes
The influenza bug a temperature high as hell
Sweating chilled to bone I'd say goodbye fair world farewell

I could get knocked o'er by a Barton bus could be
No others hurt along the road only there just me
Maybe I'll fall down a cliff my namesake yea a fall
I wonder if I'll hear owt the holy trumpet call

I don't imagine I'll be missed a mess I've made of life
A bad un most of all it caused misery and strife
I must admit I can't predict I'll have to do me sums
Hang on a mo.... just had thought
Tomorrow never comes

I'm Sure He Would Again

With trials I know you're with me
I can feel it in my heart
This feeling is never ending
Now I will praise you from the start
I can hear you knocking
I will let you in
Now my heart is open
My healing can begin
Everlasting Father
Jesus was your aim
You died to save us
I'm sure you would again

Jesus died to save us
I'm sure he would again
Now that you are with me
My path is made clear
To follow in your righteousness
My soul will never fear
Your Love is everlasting and
Clear for me to see
I hope I will never lose you
Or stray too far away

Pandemic

Battle through nothing else to do
111 you may as well ring Tom Thumb
As passed back to GP, to see if you're worthy of help
If your Data does not fit, stay at home stay safe
Sore throat, coughing nothing is working
Sick of taking things and still hurting
No help or so it seems, from this Great Britain a bygone dream

Maintain what's there or so they say, dilapidation is here to stay
No more Great this country once was,
when God was at the forefront and
People gave a toss. Think of self
and none other let them poor people die in the gutter.
Where is the Love for our fellow Man?

Broken and Hurting

I am broken and hurting
Battered and bruised
The things that I've been through
Leave me feeling confused

I have lived for your glory
Sacrificed self
And I thought in my story
All would end well

I looked and I waited
For a change to occur
I prayed and I fasted
Never murmured a word

But the change never happened
Things only got worse
Was it me? I was saddened
Was I under a curse?

As I took all the blame
For the things that were wrong
Was it always a game?
For the truth I did long

But the truth as it dawned
Felt as hard as the lie
From my youth I'd been conned
It was time to say bye

And your word never faltered
As you led me to peace
My theology you altered
Took apart piece by piece

Now I'm living my life
In the truth of your word
Although there is strife
And life may seem absurd

I am loved and I'm heard
My value immense
Though my name may be slurred
You will be my defence

I am broken and hurting
Battered and bruised
But the things I have been through
Led me closer to you

Past and Present

I tried the drug amphetamine
For years would I race
I tried opiate heroine
To slow down and ease my pace

I tried the reefer cannabis
To seek wisdom could I find
I tried the licit alcohol
To get blottoed out of mind
I tried those upper downers
Barbituates and all
I tried to be a hard man
No withdrawal just stand tall
I tried the white powder
The one they call cocaine

But later found no family
Just anguish, raging pain
I cheated and I lied through life
A criminal a thug
I paid the price with sentences
The holes I've toiled so dug
Then change came into self
So seems a church I sought the truth
In Christ our Saviour wisdom found
In I am living proof
I found a grace without a growl
A sympathy a love
I saw my Christ a living Lord

A light shone high above
I found a bond with He alone
Which gave me inner peace
I found no condemnation just
Forgiveness my past release
I found in times so difficult
When clasped my hands in prayer
I felt a comfort warm surround
Just knowing you were there
I found a soul which once was lost
A heart so cold and iced
I thank my Lord on bended knee
I worship You my Christ
I see your works in forest glen
In wildlife lowly wren
I close my eyes and calmly pray
To you then proudly close Amen

A Simple Favour

So here I am standing before you
With quite a story to tell
Some parts may bring a tear
Others may cause you to yell,
So where do I start…?
I was homeless and an addict
Living in chaos with no sign of a light
To guide my way out
…So I thought… But… I could never predict
How my life could transform
From the chaos out of which I was born
Perpetual violence, misery and pain
Each day so very different
Yet always still the same
My waking prayer was for me to die
And in so many ways believe me I've tried
To end my life without success
Please God let me go "I cried"
To something I didn't believe in
However I prayed all the time
For all the bad things I wanted
Little did I know of the beauty so sublime
That finally now I have found
When a friend of mine prompted
Say the sinner's prayer he said
What harm can it do…?
To a life full of blessing you will be led
But you have to want it and mean it,
Truly and honestly in your heart.

Well… if it can pull me out of this pit…
…That's tearing my life apart…
…I'll give it a go…
…Give Jesus a try…
And so I said those words,
I started to cry,
For something I felt deep inside
Something I thought was surely lost,
Now filled with love…
…Gone was my pride,
If this is how God feels…
…I'm in, no matter the cost,
And since that special day
Now with peace in my soul
Each and every day I pray
For Christ in my heart for now I am whole
So… as I go under…
…Say goodbye to the old…
For I will arise victorious…
…With a new story to be told
Washed clean of my sin
A new creation to behold
Jesus Christ you are my Saviour
I will praise you my King…
For you've made a cold heart sing…
Thanks to one act of kindness,
To him "one simple favour"
So thankyou my friend
And thank you my Jesus

For I am "A CHILD OF GOD…"

Amen

Bullied

They never come in ones or twos
There's usually three or four
They punch and kick until
Their will submitted on the floor

But harken to a tale of woe
Of a kid who knew the score
Who battled back yeah bloodied
But learned there so much more

Take out the leader watch him fall
And his minions cringe with fear
The shackles loosed within one's mind
The terror forms oh dear

A reputation battled hard
From youth to adolescence
Fear none just hurt and hunger more
No regret or recompense

They flee when eyes are glaring
When controls gone by the by
Just listen to the moans of pain
Listen to them cry

Yes mortal and feel pain intense
But let it enter in
A life snuffed out whatever done
To I there is no sin

Yes bullied drove a child to rise
To forfeit all his youth
To stand there tall unwavering
In I this is the proof
Regrets I've none I've vanquished all who stood
And said let's fight
I've delved in demons dark as coal
And summoned all my might

I've lost a lot along the way
But still I feel no wrong
The pain I've felt and suffered so
In truth has made me strong

This Warrior Cross

I hold in my hand
This reminder of how
My Saviour chose death
His pain did allow

My cross is smooth
And easy to bear
His cross was rough
There were thorns in his hair

The brass in the middle
A sword in my hand
Reminding me always
For truth we do stand

The copper reminds me
Of those needing prayer
As I touch each small circle
I pray 'cos I care

My cross is smooth
And easy to bear
His cross was rough
There were thorns in his hair

I sit in silence
Peace overshadows me
You endured mocking
As you hung on that tree

The scent of my cross
Brings joy and brings calm
The fruit of your suffering
The nails in your palms

My cross is smooth
And easy to bear
His cross was rough
There were thorns in his hair

Atonement

An accident that's all it was, I've heard so many years
The doubts in place the innocent plea, along with all their tears
A counsellor no right to judge, just listen take a seat
Then hears the explanations to harken words they bleat

And yet I should allow their thought, for the grace of God go I
They don't ask about my present past the hunger to ask why
My sins and theirs are for my Father, He is the final judge
And I must be obedient from my path I must not budge

I must walk this path I asked for, to aid oneself to build
To don my armour to protect my Master there so willed
He's never put me wrong in life He's listened to my woe
He lifted carried cradled enabling me to grow

He's given gifts unknowing, for I to cherish hone
And for my past forgiven, myself I must atone
I thank you oh my Father your Son and Holy Ghost
Although I've given up the drink, with cup of tea I'll toast

Life Story

Stiff necked so proud I do no wrong
Get out vile creature where you belong
No evil thought no downcast deed
I talk so open folk to feed

No despise of any just love for all
I walk through life so upright tall
I consider self but no gossip spite
I wander soul so pure and right

I do not tote one envious bone
To none or any I must atone
I walk a Christian path of hope
No pretence or con

No words soft soap
So pure am I my smile is good
I kneel to pray drink of His blood
I eat my worth of body Christ

No chill of soul
No heat so iced

None can claim a bad bone have I
No need to whisper gossip pry
My goodness shines from inside out
I do not drink belligerent shout

I'm honest proud reliable true
Always happy never blue
And then I stand and take a peek
My inside pain still there so bleak

I'll put on show pretend awhile
It'll go away put clothes on style
And when I face my master there
He'll love me still, show kindness care

He'll ask me why I lived such hell
When all it took a friend to tell
I'll talk with He and find release
My soul and mind will be at peace

Life's Past

I knew a man; this man would fight in anger there he'd sneer
He'd take drugs to compensate, drink copious amounts of beer.
I knew this man from inside out, or so I'd ponder thought
I saw him prisoned for his crimes, in times when he'd been caught.

I saw him brave the vicious cries, of bastards to the realm
He lived behind a wall of steel, like one captain at his helm
I knew this giant man of worth, of values far beyond
Then yet he could not understand, to talk or correspond

I knew not of control inside, and yet I knew his flaws
I could perceive one loving gift,
from behind his closed locked doors
I knew a man, a man that was, for now a vision's sought
With help from peoples black and white,
to these future realms been brought

I knew a man, a man that was,
with taught wisdom he now can see
I know the treasures of his soul,
for in truth that man was me

Fifty

Fifty is a looming it's enough to make you spit
Our bodies are about knackered with so many years to live.

We take for granted when in our youth
that our bodies will be fine
Like walking out in winter with scarcely nothing on and
Drinking till we're sober and think it's just all fun,

Our bodies they creak now, our muscles hurt all the time
Is it because of what we've done with our bodies in our time?

Maybe we could get fit now and go to the gym
Put ourselves through more pain to feel better within
Or are we content with how we feel within?

We only know the truth as no one else can see in
But there is one who sees and knows our deepest within
Who always wants the best for us and never to give in?

The family He created to Love each other so
To help each other freely and let each other grow
So I'm glad we have our family although none are the same,
To share our Love intently to watch each other flow

You are the God...

You are the God who heals
Nothing is hidden
All is revealed
You are the God who heals

You are the God who loves
Unconditional
All accepting
You are the God who loves

You are the God never changing
Yesterday
Today and forever
You are the God never changing

You are the God Almighty
Sovereign, All powerful
Just and yet merciful
You are the God almighty

You are the God who is personal
Heavenly Father
My friend and my brother
You are the God who is personal

Disfigured

Who states in life we cannot do
Who shackles being held?
With talents all we have inside
Could tell a tale be-spelled
Who says our traits?? Disabled
We cannot ne'er perform

And yet our sense for human race
Its tender spirit warm
Who then can hold this spirit ripe?
We can in fact achieve
Our forms may be disfigured
Hence paralysed we cannot breath

We are, we can, we shall
We see all fellows womankind
We shout we do we will be heard
Not left alone behind

We're equal on this planet
Round we sense, we feel, we see
No special treatment do we need
No apologies for me

I am this person body form
No matter of my ails
I have some sort of illness
Just ask it's all entails

But see me as a person
Dyslexic word or number
But I will try my damnedest
Best my form will not encumber

Now look upon this person
Emotions just like you
I think myself so privileged
To live to full so true
My personage as everyone
Is differed as a print

And sometimes yes I overspend
Pockets empty there I'm skint
So come I have explained my form
And also stated time
Now look upon with altered view
In fact it is but me

Faith

Beyond all your transgressions
Made transcripts poems and games you've played
Beyond deceit and lies untold
Lives web of coins at end unfold

Beyond our realms of lives said
Plain truth curdled thought, downpour it rains
Beyond a snigger implied unsaid
One's moral code of life is read

Beyond the secrets kept from man
Through portalled eyes the true life span

Beyond our reach to stars above
Our hopes and dreams in spiralled love
Beyond the masks of features cold
Through granite rock one's story told

Beyond our breath we hold so dear
The seconds pass our path is clear
Beyond so far beyond we see a gate
Inscribed our name to be

Beyond the pain of laboured birth
Our eyes are clear at last we see

Beyond our souls of rewards we sort a trap unseen
We're snagged and caught
Beyond our cravings for perfect peace we soar again so free release
Beyond the pangs of guilt and hell
We form a bond long past foretell

Beyond our parenthood practised fore
We smell the stench of bloodied gore
Beyond our meagre strengths behaved
We found once lost a man be saved

Just Water

The tears cascade in torrents
Form a salty stream on face
Then all emotions ease and cease
They're gone without a trace

These feelings deep I crush and harden
for a man must never cry
He's tough and strong nothing endures
He'll never question why

The years roll on and on and on
To a plain where no one's been
I've travelled over countless eons
And logged what I have seen

This pain ensued through all those years
but cause a lot well sorta
The people smirk and smile
At tears a statement loud just water

The decades of one's life of hope
Dashed smashed one's heart torn out
Stand alone in silent room
Let none see kick or shout

The people do not want to look
They do not want to spy despair
They watch the telly have a laugh
All controlled from out of one's chair

The rat race rushes hither to hither
Yon no one sees or gives a care
They walk away then feel the guilt
So sometimes state who's there

The people give their sound advice
If you did or didn't oughta
The pain inside is just as fierce
But to the hordes it is just water

Standing in Line

Standing patiently in line
My Pride is on the floor
I'm Trying not to think
And I'm Trying not to feel

How did I get here?
I don't think I belong
Fighting back the fear
Trying to stay strong

The line is moving forward
Another one goes in
Why do I feel awkward?
Like I've lived a life of sin?

How did I get here?
I don't think I belong
Fighting back the fear
Trying to stay strong

It's not that I'm ungrateful
In fact I'm quite relieved
To get a box of food and stuff
To meet my children's needs

How did I get here?
I don't think I belong
Fighting back the fear
Trying to stay strong

My stomach feels uneasy
The tears I'm holding back
This wasn't what I ever dreamed
My life has gone off track

From That Day

From the day my heart opened and I let you in
That was the day all my sins you paid for all of them
I'm always thinking how I'm born again
Past behind me, now I'm living with the truth within

With my life you now lead
Sometimes all I need
new thoughts you set the seed
Sometimes all I need
your guiding path I follow forth
Sometimes all I need
the wisdom of your voice

The prince of peace
Where living in your wake
Humble healer changing lives through your faith
Holy proclaimer we will stand
Walking forward you said to me
I am your God so don't be afraid
your place is here with me.

Demons

You became a changeling to transform corrupt inflict transgress
Havoc was your middle name, to instruct in chaos mess
You altered shape and time to suit, involving millions to one's cause
Never faltered from one's task, alienated without a pause
You savaged searched and brutalised, and did so with a smile
You took your snares in ambush terms, and waited for a while

You scorched the earth with pestilence,
crushed all beneath one's feet
Drained and ravished all with sustenance
then listened to them bleat

You wandered over centuries through portals time and space
Attaching with a cunning style, to pillage human race
You manipulated all emotions anger, guilt, and shame
To prove a point of evidence that life is just a game

Your vengeance could ne'er be quenched you bled the victims dry
And never once you sort your soul, to question asking why
Then ask yourself in simple truth
without ploys and plans to scheme
Was your pain so dreadful then or a splinter from a beam?

Broken

I think I'm broken
Got it wrong
misunderstanding
The wrong song

Thought my suffering
Was for a cause
Thought my faith came
With a clause

Accept mistreatment
Must endure
All for Jesus
Save our souls

Scripture twisted
Been made captive
Look for freedom
Can't stay passive

Imagine

Just imagine what He went through to cleanse this world from sin
His statements not condemning be kind to kith and kin
The hunger that he must have felt for forty days and nights
The battles with the enemy, for love, our human rights

He made a blind man see again, a cripple to stand tall
Destroyed those table taxes in temple's marbled hall
Water into wine He made, a festival of love
Three fish and some loaves of bread all manna from above

His faith in God did not falter as they lashed Him with a whip
The thorns forced upon His precious head,
His blood down face did drip
They nailed His hands and feet to cross, His Father poured out scorn
His promise for His sacrifice is all can be reborn

Guard my Heart

Empty promises
Lies, deceit
Truth is twisted
Your needs to meet

Words mean nothing
All an act
Sounds convincing
Spoke as fact

Truth is harder
To discern
Listen closely
You will learn

Attitudes held
Haven't shifted
Sense of entitlement
Hasn't lifted

And so I know
I must stay strong
Guard my heart
You don't belong

The Complexity of Love

We only see what we wish to see
until we look deeper into Love

Look at the Lover and how He Loves us
and our Love for Him will grow

Dancing from hate and wasted through grief,
change to see, to see it

Laugh in the Love warm and tender,
to identify Him in the Spirit

Look for His healing hands

We forget how much He Loves us,
we forget how much He cares

If He said he wanted to go to the deepest point of us
would we be scared?

God Loves us so dearly, there is no need to be scared.

'You are the God who heals
Nothing is hidden'